Early Intermediate
Intermediate

AN COATES

HILARIOUS

POPULAR PIANO LIBRARY

BOOK 2

CONTENTS

ISBN-10: 0-7390-5335-3
ISBN-13: 978-0-7390-5335-8

Alfred

THE ABA-DABA HONEYMOON

Words and Music by
Arthur Fields and Walter Donovan
Arranged by Dan Coates

BARNEY GOOGLE

Words and Music by
Billy Rose and Con Conrad
Arranged by Dan Coates

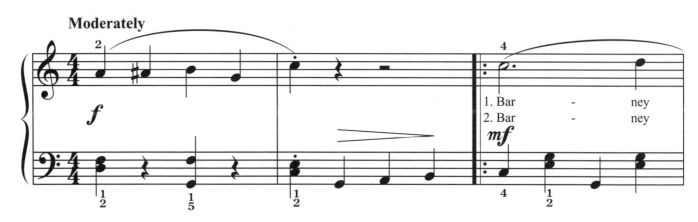

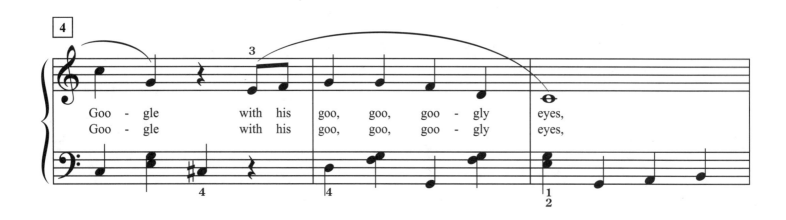

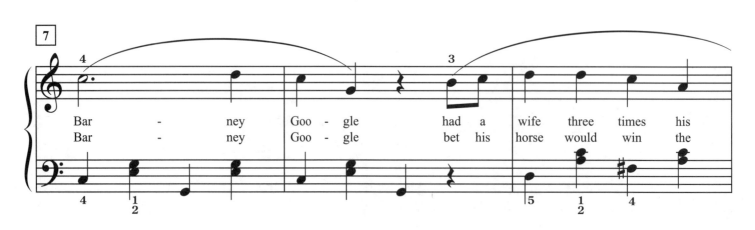

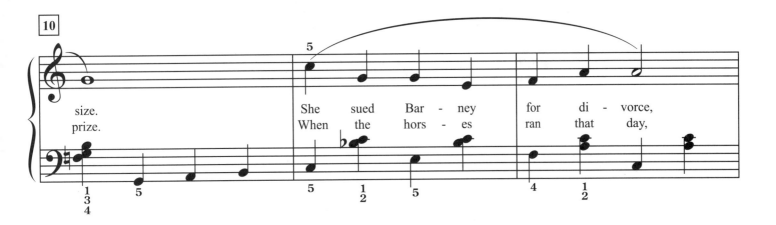

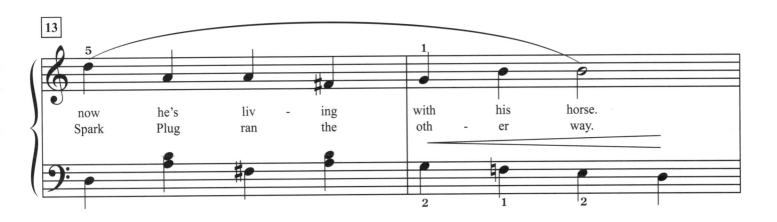

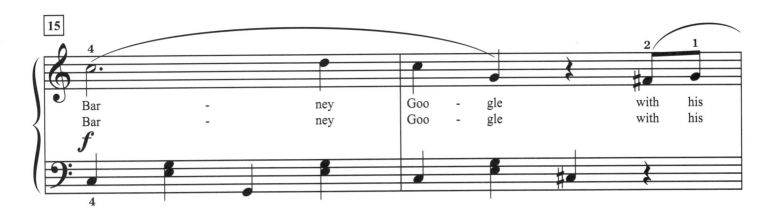

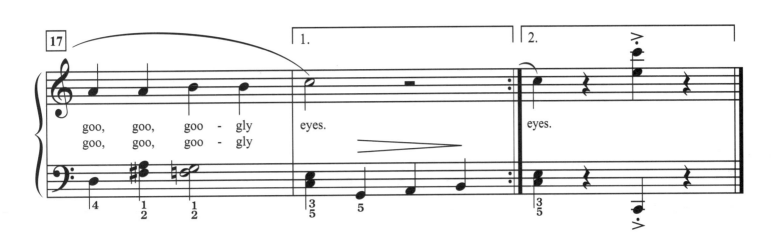

BE MY LITTLE BABY BUMBLEBEE

Words and Music by
Stanley Murphy and Henry I. Marshall
Arranged by Dan Coates

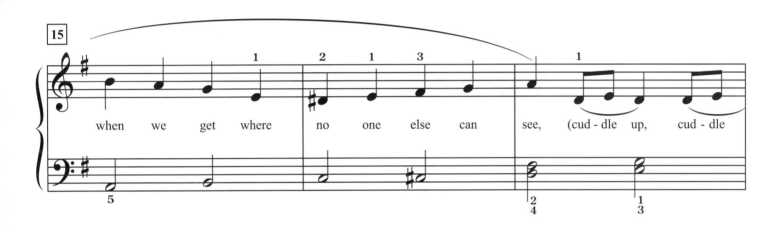

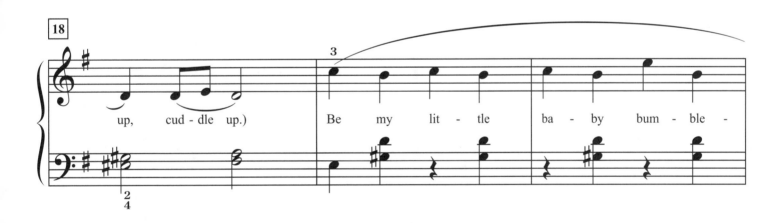

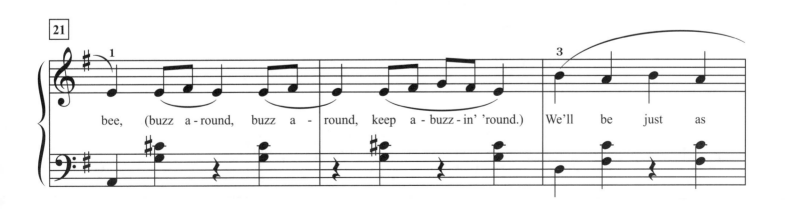

hap - py   as   can   be,   (you and me,   you and   me,   you and me.)

cresc.

Hon - ey,   keep   a - buzz - in'   please,   I've   got   a   doz - en

cou - sin   bees,   but I   want   you   to   be my   ba - by   bum - ble -

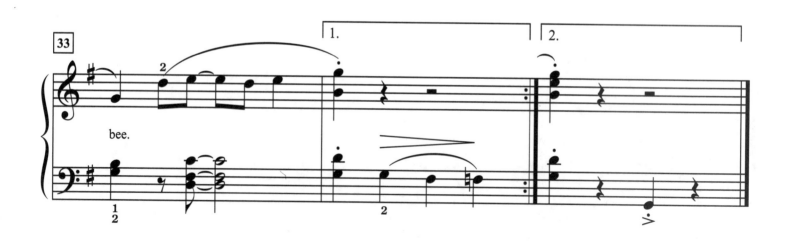

bee.

CHEESEBURGER IN PARADISE

Words and Music by Jimmy Buffett
Arranged by Dan Coates

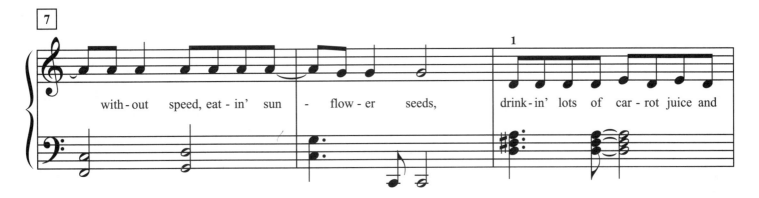

DO YOUR EARS HANG LOW?

Traditional
Arranged by Dan Coates

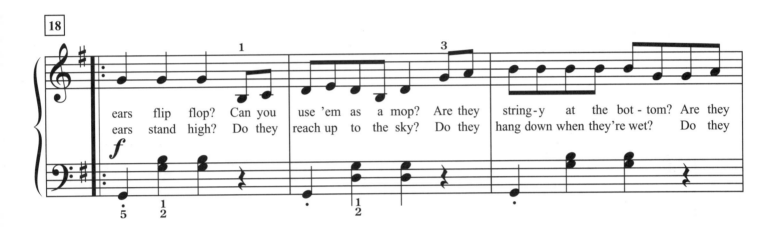

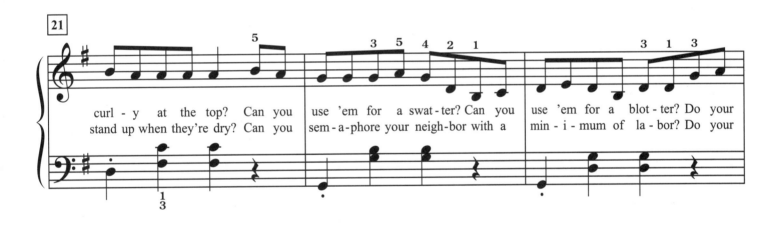

DOES YOUR CHEWING GUM LOSE ITS FLAVOR ON THE BEDPOST OVERNIGHT?

Words and Music by Billy Rose,
Marty Bloom and Ernest Breuer
Arranged by Dan Coates

DOODLE DOO DOO

Words and Music by
Art Kassel and Mel Stitzel
Arranged by Dan Coates

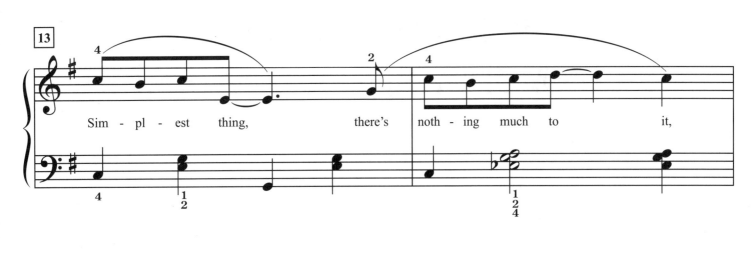

Sim - pl - est thing, there's noth - ing much to it,

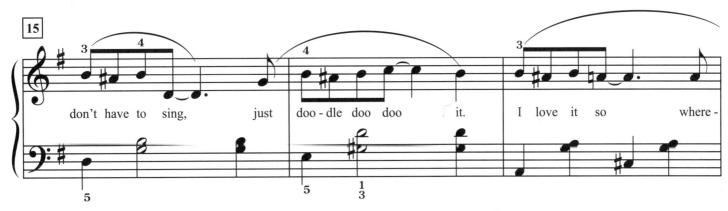

don't have to sing, just doo - dle doo doo it. I love it so where -

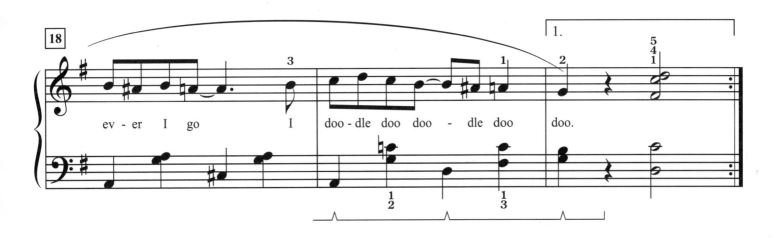

ev - er I go I doo - dle doo doo - dle doo doo.

doo - dle doo doo - dle doo, doo - dle - doo doo - dle doo doo!

HELLO MUDDAH, HELLO FADDUH!

Music by Lou Busch
Words by Allan Sherman
Arranged by Dan Coates

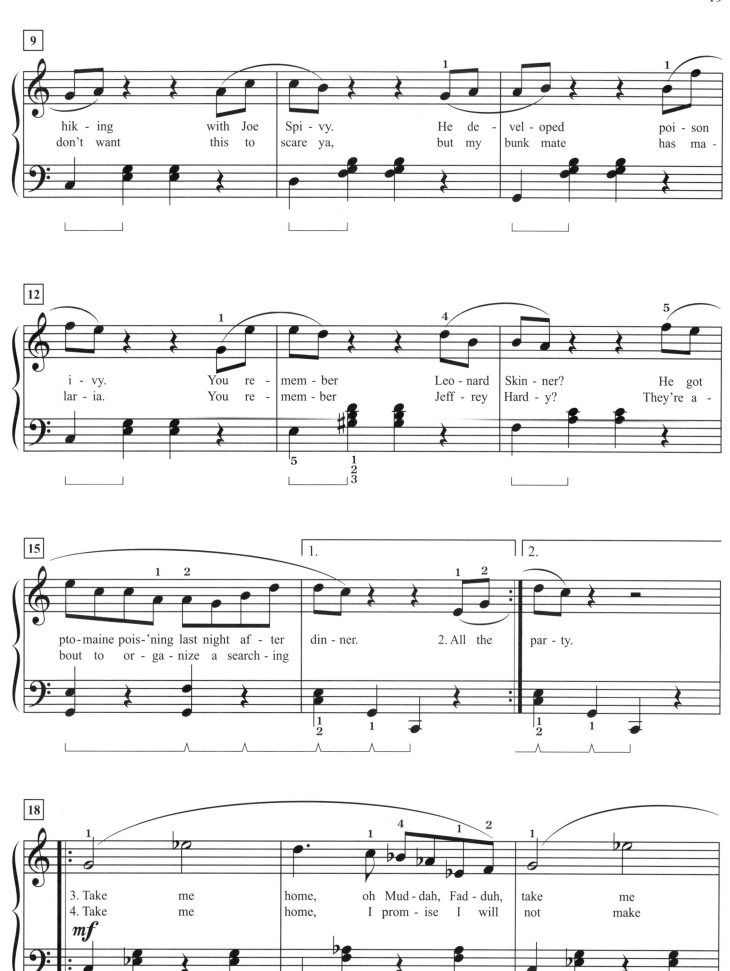

home, I hate Gra - na - da. Don't leave me out in the for - est
noise or mess the house with oth - er boys. Oh, please don't make me

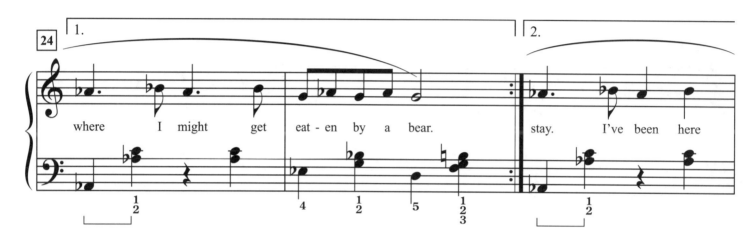

where I might get eat - en by a bear.
stay. I've been here

one whole day. Dear - est Fad - duh, dar - ling Mud - dah, how's my

pre - cious lit - tle brud - dah? Let me come home if you

miss me. I would e - ven let Aunt Ber - tha hug and kiss me. Wait a

min - ute, it stopped hail - ing. Guys are swim - ming, guys are

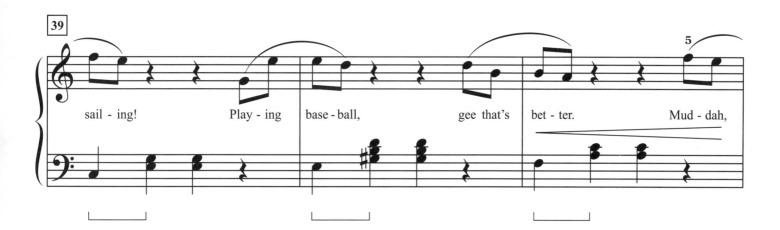

sail - ing! Play - ing base - ball, gee that's bet - ter. Mud - dah,

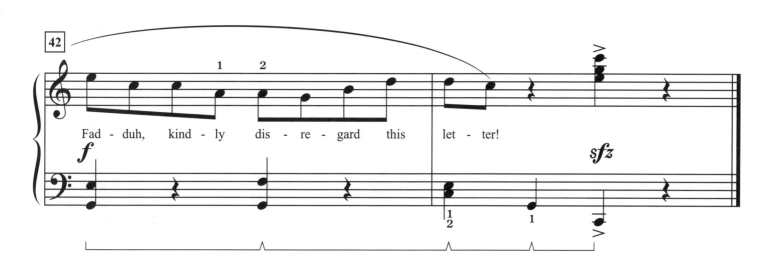

Fad - duh, kind - ly dis - re - gard this let - ter!

THE CHICKEN DANCE (DANCE LITTLE BIRD)

Music by Terry Rendall and Werner Thomas
English Lyrics by Paul Parnes
Arranged by Dan Coates

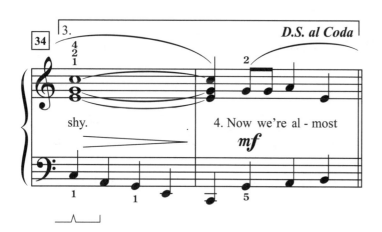

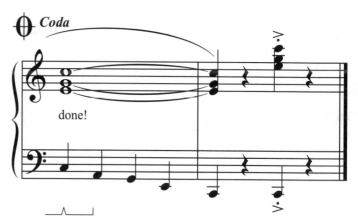

Verse 2:
Hey, you're in the swing.
You're cluckin' like a bird. (Pluck, pluck, pluck, pluck.)
You're flappin' your wings.
Don't you feel absurd? (No, no, no, no.)
It's a chicken dance,
Like a rooster and a hen. (Ya, ya, ya, ya.)
Flappy chicken dance,
Let's do it again. *(To Chorus 2:)*

Chorus 2:
Relax and let the music move you.
Let all your inhibitions go.
Just watch your partner whirl around you.
We're having fun now, I told you so.

Verse 3:
Now you're flapping like a bird
And you're wigglin' too. (I like that move.)
You're without a care.
It's a dance for you. (Just made for you.)
Keep doin' what you do.
Don't you cop out now. (Don't you cop out now.)
Gets better as you dance,
Catch your breath somehow. *(To Chorus 3:)*

Verse 4:
Now we're almost through,
Really flyin' high. (Bye, bye, bye, bye.)
All you chickens and birds,
Time to say goodbye. (To say goodbye.)
Goin' back to the nest,
But the flyin' was fun. (Oh, it was fun.)
Chicken dance was the best,
But the dance is done!

ITSY BITSY TEENIE WEENIE YELLOW POLKA DOT BIKINI

Words and Music by
Paul J. Vance and Lee Pockriss
Arranged by Dan Coates

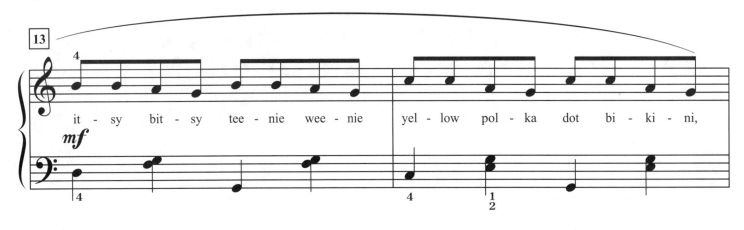

it - sy bit - sy tee - nie wee - nie yel - low pol - ka dot bi - ki - ni,

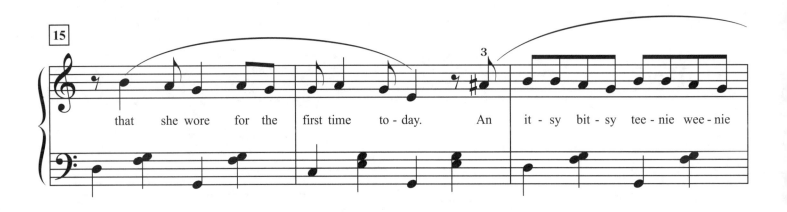

that she wore for the first time to - day. An it - sy bit - sy tee - nie wee - nie

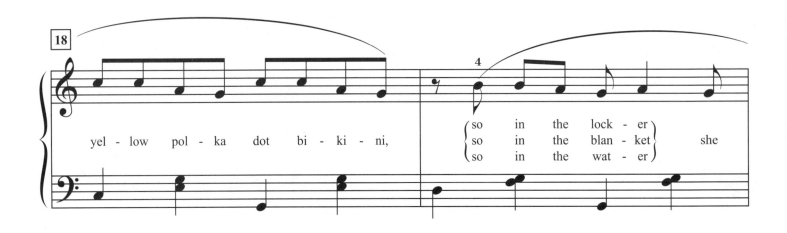

yel - low pol - ka dot bi - ki - ni,
{ so in the lock - er }
{ so in the blan - ket } she
{ so in the wat - er }

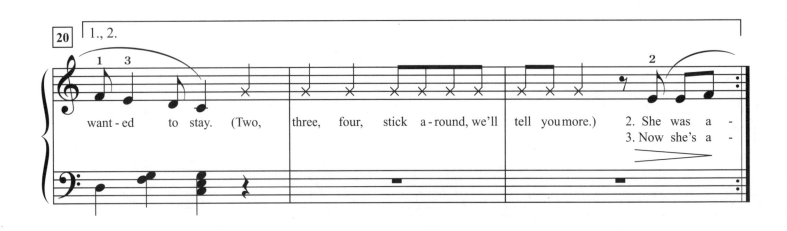

want - ed to stay. (Two, three, four, stick a - round, we'll tell you more.) 2. She was a -
3. Now she's a -

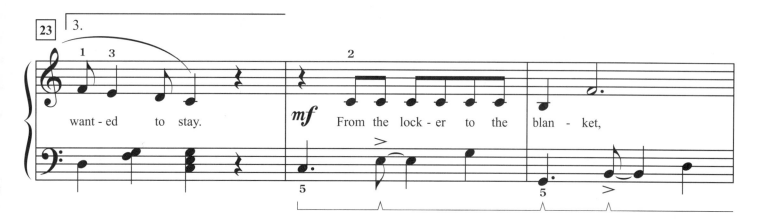

want - ed to stay. *mf* From the lock - er to the blan - ket,

from the blan - ket to the shore. From the shore to the

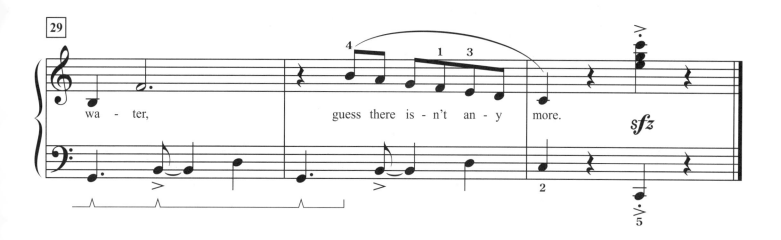

wa - ter, guess there is - n't an - y more. *sfz*

Verse 2:
She was afraid to come out in the open,
And so a blanket around her she wore.
She was afraid to come out in the open,
And so she sat bundled up on the shore.
(Two, three, four, tell the people what she wore.)

Verse 3:
Now she's afraid to come out of the water,
And I wonder what she's gonna do.
Now she's afraid to come out of the water,
And the poor little girl's turning blue.
(Two, three, four, tell the people what she wore.)

JEEPERS CREEPERS

Words by Johnny Mercer
Music by Harry Warren
Arranged by Dan Coates

TALK TO THE ANIMALS

Words and Music by Leslie Bricusse
Arranged by Dan Coates

flea.

We would con - verse in po - lar bear and

mp

py - thon,

and we would curse in flu - ent kan - ga -

roo.

mf

If peo - ple asked us, "Can you speak rhi -

noc - er - ous?"

cresc.

We'd say, "Of cours - er - ous!

Can't

you?"

f *mf*

If we con - ferred with our fur - ry friends,